Indiana

Thomas G Aylesworth
Virginia L Aylesworth

Photos by
John R Savage

BLUE CROSS—BLUE SHIELD

MNB

Bison Books

First published in 1985 by
Bison Books Ltd
176 Old Brompton Road
London SW5
England

ISBN 0 86124 240 8

Printed in Hong Kong

Dedication

For Jack K Overmyer, a great newspaperman and good friend

Acknowledgments

The authors and publisher would like to thank the following people who have helped in the
preparation of this book: Blackbirch Graphics, who designed it; Elizabeth M Montgomery,
who edited it; Mary R Raho, who selected the pictures.

Photo Credits

All photographs were taken by John R Savage, with the following exceptions:
Anderson/Madison County Visitor and Convention Bureau: 87 (top).
FPG: 2-3, 4-5, 88-89.
Indiana Department of Commerce: 16 (center right), 21 (bottom right), 25 (top), 39
(bottom), 42 (left), 48, 51 (right), 52-53, 59 (top), 60 (bottom), 64 (bottom right), 69 (top),
70, 72 (top left), 79 (top), 81, 82 (bottom left), 84-85, 95 (bottom).

Contents

Introduction

To heaven raise thy star-crowned head,
Superb Indiana.
Thy future to glory wed . . .

That's what we learned in elementary school—'The Hymn to Indiana.' And we believed it and still do.

Indiana—'The Crossroads of America.' Indiana—'The Hoosier State.' What better place to grow up—a state with a glorious past and an unlimited future.

They called it Indiana—'The Land of Indians'—and certainly the Indians were there first. In the beginning were the prehistoric mound builders, and their village sites can still be seen in the state. When the two French explorers, Father Marquette and Louis Joliet, arrived in northern Indiana in 1673 to preach to the Indians, and when the Frenchman Robert Cavelier, Sieur de La Salle, came from Canada in 1679 for his six-year exploration of the area, they found only a few hundred Indians, most of them from the Miami tribe.

In the 1700s and early 1800s, Indiana was home to dispossessed Eastern tribes, such as the Delaware, Mohican, Munsee, Shawnee, Huron, Kickapoo, Piankashaw, Potawatomi and Wea. By 1838, however, most had moved again; the Potawatomi sold their land to the government and the rest had been driven out by military force.

During the 1720s, the French built fur-trading posts at Miami (near Fort Wayne) and Ouiatenon (near Lafayette), and founded a fort at Vincennes, the state's oldest settlement, in 1732.

Then came the British, who competed with the French for furs, and defeated the French in 1763, who ceded the lands to the British. During the Revolutionary War, George Rogers Clark took Vincennes in 1779, winning for the United States what was called the Northwest Territory. Vincennes became the capital of that territory—which included Indiana, Illinois and Wisconsin and part of Michigan and Minnesota. On 11 December 1816 Indiana joined the Union as the nineteenth state and Jonathan Jennings, a Democratic-Republican, became its first governor. At the time it had but 64,000 people.

Top: The peony—the state flower of Indiana.
Left: The Convent of the Immaculate Conception in Ferdinand, Dubois County.

Page 1: The Indiana state flag flies proudly beneath the Stars and Stripes.
Previous spread: Covered bridges cross many of Indiana's rivers and streams.

Glorious fall foliage near a farm pond.

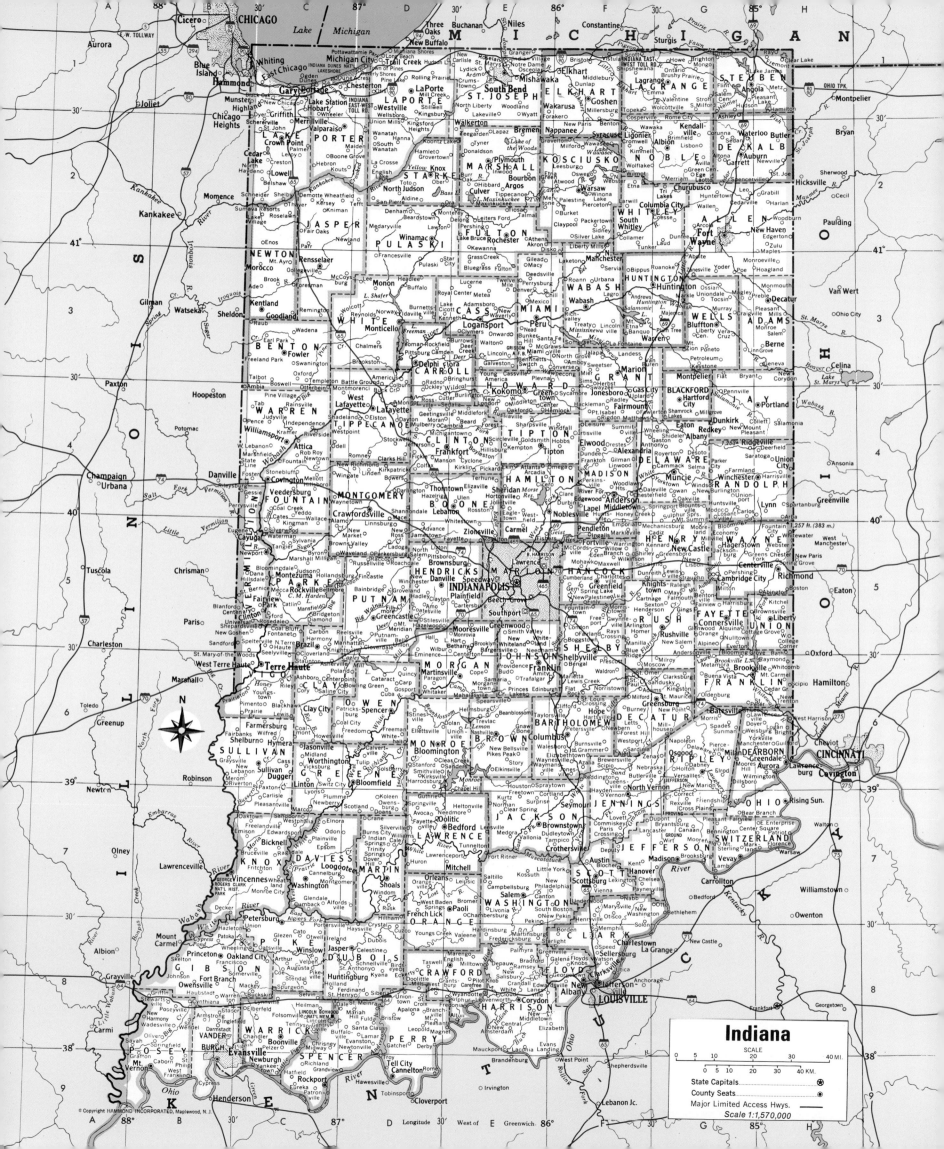

Indiana

SCALE
0 5 10 20 30 40 MI.
0 5 10 20 30 40 KM.

State Capitals .... ⊛
County Seats .... ●
Major Limited Access Hwys. .... ▬▬

Scale 1:1,570,000

A Land of
Beauty

A Land of **Beauty**

Indiana the beautiful. More beautiful than most because it offers three different kinds of beauty to appreciate. There is beauty in the Great Lakes Plains that stretch across the northern border and extend south for about 60 miles to the south. This is the land of lakes, small hills and rock left by departing glaciers. There is beauty in the Till Plains of the central part of the state. Here is found the Indiana part of the great Midwestern Corn Belt, with its rich soil, low hills and broad, shallow valleys. There is beauty in the southern hills and lowlands, which extend from the Ohio River on the south in a bellshaped curve from New Harmony up around Bloomington and back down to the river near Madison. This is the land which the ancient glaciers did not reach—the land of steep hills and limestone.

More than 130 kinds of trees are indigenous to Indiana, not to mention the recently introduced species such as, for example, the ginkgo on the Indiana University campus. The most common are ash, beech, black walnut, various kinds of maple and oak, bog willow, elm, sycamore, tamarack and the yellow poplar (or tulip tree, Indiana's state tree). Black gum, pawpaw, persimmon, southern cypress and Virginia pine are also to be found. And in the fall, when the deciduous trees change color, the foliage rivals the beauty of any other part of the United States.

The variety of the smaller plant life is astonishing. There are prickly-pear cactus plants and orchids to be found in the dunes region of the northwest. There are floating pondweeds and pepper-mints in the lake region in the north, as well as insect-eating plants such as the bladderwort, the sundew and the pitcher plant. When spring comes, the spicy scent of the state flower, the peony, fills the air, as does that of the lilac. In the summer, the pussy willows, the sweet clover, the oxeye daisies, the corn cockle and the Queen Anne's lace appear. In autumn come the asters, fringed gentians, goldenrod and sunflowers.

Some of the native animals to be seen are muskrats, opossums, raccoons, skunks and woodchucks. There are yellow-winged sparrows, prairie larks, wood thrushes, blue jays, orioles, swallows, quail, pheasant, wrens and the cardinal, the state bird.

Top: Wyandotte Cave in Crawford County is the third largest in the United States.
Left: The seven pillars along the Mississinewa River near Peru.

Previous Spread: The Bridgeton Bridge in Parke County, where so many covered bridges are to be found.

Above: A waterfall in McCormick's Creek State Park, near Spencer. The creek plunges through a limestone canyon to join the White River.

The park contains Wolf Cave and a stone bridge over McCormick's Creek as well as steep ravines, stone gullies and beautiful forests.

Right: An intriguing trail through the beech and pines in 'Mac's Creek.'

Top: The Great Mound in the rolling woodlands of Mounds State Park, near Anderson. The 259-acre park preserves the earth formations built many centuries ago by the prehistoric mound-building Indians.
Above: The Indiana Dunes State Park, near Chesterton, contains beautiful white sand dunes and beaches that stretch for three miles along Lake Michigan's south shore. The 1800 acres of the park contain densely-forested hills that, with their wide variety of flowers and ferns, look almost tropical in the summer.
Left: A trail in Turkey Run State Park, near Marshall. The park is a 2382-acre tract of beautiful virgin woods, prehistoric canyons and winding streams that twist through rock.
Opposite: Clifty Falls State Park, near Madison, contains 1360 acres on a high wooded plateau which offers magnificent views of the Ohio River.

The sunset casts its glow on the waters of the Ohio River near the town of Madison.

Top: A typical country landscape in Miami County in the Till Plains of Indiana famous for their rich farming soil.
Above: The Indiana Dunes National Lakeshore on Lake Michigan contains 8239 acres of beautiful beaches.
Left: Winters can be fierce in Indiana, especially in the northern snow belt. But there is beauty to be seen, as in this winter scene near Akron.
Right: An early morning view along a trail in Pokagon State Park, which is located on the shores of Lake James and Snow Lake near Angola.

A Land of History

A Land of **History**

When Indiana became a state in 1816, its capital was at Corydon, just a few miles north of the Ohio River. In 1818, the Federal Government bought the central part of the state and after this 'New Purchase,' turned it over to the state. This meant that settlers began arriving in the central area, and by 1820 they began to arrive in an area that was to become Indianapolis—right in the center of the state. This seemed a sensible spot for a state capital, and in 1825 the state offices were moved there from Corydon. It wasn't until 1847 that Indianapolis was incorporated as a city.

During the 1850s, the railroads began pushing into Indiana. And cities began to grows as industry began to become prominent. Clement and Henry Studebaker opened a blacksmith and wagon shop in South Bend in 1852, which first became a wagon manufacturing shop and then an automobile factory. Richard Gatling developed his machine gun in Indianapolis in 1862 and James Oliver invented the hard-steel plow in Indiana in the 1860s. In the energy field, the first gasoline pump was manufactured in Fort Wayne in 1885 (when Henry Ford was only 22 years old), natural gas was discovered near Portland in 1886 and Standard Oil built one of the world's first oil refineries in Whiting in 1889.

By the turn of the century, about one-third of the population of the state had moved to the cities and Indiana was beginning to turn the corner from being a rural state to an urban one. Today, almost 70 percent of the population lives in cities.

The Hoosier State has changed, but one thing remains constant. No one really knows how it got its nickname. Some say that a contractor on the Ohio Falls Canal at Louisville, Samuel Hoosier, in 1826 gave employment preference to men living on the Indiana side of the Ohio River. These men became 'Hoosier's Men.' Others maintain that it stems from the answer that southern Indianians gave to a knock at the door of their log cabins in the middle of the night—'Who's Here?' An even more farfetched idea is the one in which an Indiana man, excited about the valor of a certain type of European solider, beat up on a bully and shouted, 'I'm a Hoosier' —meaning a Hussar. No matter where the origin, Indiana people use the name with pride.

Top: A scene from 'The Feast of the Hunters' Moon' at Fort Ouiatenon at Lafayette—a celebration of the fall season as it was 200 years ago.

Left: The 'Trail of Courage Rendezvous' at Rochester—a commemoration of the courage of the Potawatomi Indians in their forced march to Kansas.
Previous spread: Billie Creek Village near Rockville—a re-creation of a turn-of-the century Indiana village, complete with stores and houses.

Top: The 100 Center Complex in Mishawaka is a nostalgic preservation area with 35 shops, restaurants and a theater, plus a brewery of the 1850s.

Above: Buildings in the Pioneer Village in Spring Mill State Park near Mitchell, an early trading post, now a restoration containing a gristmill that dates from 1816, shops and houses.

Left: St Francis Xavier Cathedral, a minor basilica, in Vincennes, was built in 1826. Its parish is the oldest in Indiana—1749.

Right: The oldest church in Indianapolis is Christ Church Cathedral. Located on Monument Circle, it was built in 1859.

Below: The old gristmill in Spring Mill State Park (1816), located in a small valley among wooded hills in this 1319-acre park. A small stream trickling through the valley turns an overshot waterwheel.

Above: The oldest surviving log house in the state of Indiana—built in 1775 in New Harmony. The town was settled by members of the Harmony Society in 1814. They preached equality, mutual protection, common ownership of property and celibacy.

Right: Historic Fort Wayne—a reconstruction of the old fort built in the period between 1815-19.
Below: Dormitory Number 2 at New Harmony. Built in 1822, it is the finest surviving example of Harmonist brick institutional architecture. Members of the Harmony Society lived here.

To the left is the Indiana Territorial Capitol of the Northwest Territory at Vincennes (1800-1813); center is Grouseland—William Henry Harrison's mansion; right is a replica of the newspaper printing shop where the *Indiana Gazette*, Indiana's first newspaper, was printed beginning in 1804.

Above: A view of Brandywine Creek at Greenfield. James Whitcomb Riley, immortalized this spot in his 'The Old Swimmin' Hole.'

Opposite top: The restored Amish homestead and farm at Nappanee.
Opposite bottom: Hook's Historical Drug Store—State Fairgrounds.

A Land of Homes

A Land of Homes

Indiana has always been a state where the people have a sense of family. When the composer wrote 'Then I long for my Indiana Home' in his song 'Back Home Again in Indiana,' he was only echoing what every Hoosier has in his or her heart—Home. And there have been a multitude of people who called Indiana 'Home.'

Presidents have lived there—Abraham Lincoln, William Henry Harrison and Benjamin Harrison—as have Nobel prize-winners—Harold Urey, Hermann J Muller, James D Watson and Salvador Luria—and astronauts Frank Borman and Virgil 'Gus' Grissom.

Native sons and daughters have made tremendous contributions to literature. Among them are Theodore Dreiser, Lloyd C Douglas, Janet Flanner, Gene Stratton Porter, Ross Lockridge, George Jean Nathan, Ernie Pyle, James Whitcomb Riley, Rex Stout, Booth Tarkington, Kurt Vonnegut, Dan Wakefield, Lew Wallace and Jessamyn West. The world of music has been influenced by native Hoosiers Hoagy Carmichael, Cole Porter, Ned Rorem, Eddie Condon, Paul Dresser and even Phil Harris and Michael Jackson.

Indiana has also produced more than its fair share of humorists, such as George Ade, Will Cuppy, Don Herold, Kin Hubbard, Emily Kimbrough, Red Skelton, Jean Shepherd and David Letterman. And what would the world of radio and television have been like without Elmer Davis, Frank Reynolds and Jane Pauley?

Indiana has been the home to social visionaries such as Eugene V Debs, Robert Owen, Father George Rapp and Wendell Willkie. Giants of industry have grown up in the Hoosier State, such as Elwood Haynes and the Studebaker Brothers, pioneer automobile builders; Richard Gatling, inventor of the Gatling gun; James Oliver, inventor of the hard-steel plow; Philo T Farnsworth, manufacturer of radios and Eli Lilly, the genius of pharmaceuticals.

But most of all, Indiana is the home of people of courage whose names have been forgotten—pioneers who tamed the wilderness; abolitionists before the Civil War who helped slaves escape to start a new, free life; crusading newspaper editors who resisted the incursions of the Ku Klux Klan; farmers who fought droughts, storms and the Great Depression to hold on to their land; factory workers who faced long hours and physical danger to produce steel.

Top: Governor William Henry Harrison built his mansion Grouseland in Vincennes in 1803-04.
Left: The Levi Coffin House in Richmond was built in 1839 in the Federal Style.

Previous spread: A magnificent old house on Anderson's historic West 8th Street—a street that contains 13 blocks of restored buildings.

Above: Benjamin Harrison's house in Indianapolis was built 15 years before he was elected President of the United States. Today it is a state memorial, containing 16 rooms with their original furniture.

Below: The 14-room cedar log house where Gene Stratton Porter lived for 20 years can be found in Limberlost State Memorial, near Geneva. She was the author of the Hoosier classic *Girl of the Limberlost*.

Above: The James Whitcomb Riley house in Indianapolis at 528 Lockerbie Street. The Hoosier Poet lived here from 1892 until 1916, and the interior has been maintained in the same condition.

Below: The Culberson Mansion in New Albany is now a state memorial. Located at 914 East Main Street, it was built in 1869 for the then astronomical cost of $120,000. Much of the interior has been restored.

Top: The General Lew Wallace house in Crawfordsville, built in 1869, was the place where this soldier, statesman, diplomat and painter wrote part of his epic novel, *Ben Hur*.
Above: Wilbur Wright was born in 1867 in this farmhouse east of New Castle.
Right: The Schofield House in Madison was built between 1809 and 1814, and is probably the first two-story tavern-house in town, built of handmade, sun-dried brick. The Federal-style structure was restored in 1975-77.
Left: The Reitz Home in Evansville (1872) is a French Second Empire mansion.

Above: The Hillforest Mansion in Aurora was built about 1852 by the industrialist, Thomas Gaff. The Italian Renaissance villa is located on 10 acres of land.
Top right: A replica of Abraham Lincoln's Indiana cabin near Lincoln City. Located nearby is the grave of his mother, Nancy Hanks Lincoln.
Center right: Governor Hendricks' house was built in Corydon in 1817 and it served as the governor's mansion from 1822-24.
Right: The Shrewsbury House in Madison has a free-standing spiral staircase (1846-1849). Madison, an old river town contains many nineteenth century houses.
Opposite: The Madison County Historic Home in Anderson was built about 1860. It has been restored and contains 12 rooms with period furnishings.

A Land of
Architecture

A Land of Architecture

Architecturally, Indiana is an eclectic state. Buildings can range from gaudy gingerbread cottages to Victorian mansions to round barns to starkly beautiful modern structures. But even the most flamboyantly ugly of the buildings, especially those built around the turn of the century, are striking and seem to have a life of their own. Hoosiers are proud of such temples as the Soldiers and Sailors Monument in Indianapolis. As any native will say, 'You might hate it, but you do have to admire it.'

Architecture styles change, and Indiana changes with them. All you have to do is to visit the campus of Indiana University to realize that. As buildings were added, the best ideas of the contemporary architects were incorporated into the planning. The result is a beautiful hodge-podge, but a hodge-podge with character, in which antique buildings stand side-by-side with modern steel and glass and beautiful Indiana limestone. It may be because of that limestone that Hoosiers accepted the changes in architectural taste. Men were cutting limestone from the Indiana quarries, knowing that this batch was going to be used in the University Union Building, while that batch was going to New York to become the Empire State Building. They learned to accept all kinds of structures.

And surely the phenomenon of Columbus is unique. Imagine a town of some 30,000 people boasting more than 40 public and private buildings designed by such notable architects as Eero Saarinen, Eliel Saarinen, John Carl Warnecke, Harry Weese, I M Pei, Kevin Roche, Eliot Noyes and J M Johansen. The whole thing started in the late 1930s when a local industrialist decided that he would pay for the services of a great architect if the builder would follow the design. Out of that simple idea came the most concentrated collection of contemporary architecture in the world, and Columbus came to be known as 'The Athens of the Midwest.'

One can stroll the street of history in Madison, with its nineteenth century houses, many of them beautifully restored. Visit covered bridges, round barns and 'castles on the hill,' view Amish farmhouses and gorgeous churches, marvel at everything from 'Steamboat Gothic' to Greek Revival to Victorian to Art Deco. Throughout its length and breadth Indiana is an architectural jewel.

Top: The unusual post office at Santa Claus. During the Christmas season several hundred thousand packages and about a million cards arrive here to be remailed with the Santa Claus, Indiana postmark.
Left: The Paxton Round Barn near Rochester, one of several barns built in this unusual shape in Fulton County.

Previous spread: The George Rogers Clark Memorial in Vincennes.

Opposite: The North Christian Church in Columbus, one of more than 40 buildings that have been designed by outstanding architects for this small town of some 30,000 people. The architect was Eero Saarinen.

Above: The Roofless Church in New Harmony, built in 1959. Designed by architect Philip Johnson, it commemorates the town's religious heritage. Inside is a Lipchitz sculpture, 'Descent of the Holy Spirit.'

Above: The Soldiers and Sailors Monument is located on Monument Circle in the heart of Indianapolis.
Left: The unique Fair Play Fire Company House is located in Madison.
Opposite top: The Wabash County Courthouse in Wabash, with the Wabash County Historical Museum to the left. On 31 March 1880, the courthouse was illuminated by four electric carbon lamps and Wabash became one of the first electrically lighted cities in the world.
Opposite bottom: A view of the verandah of the French Lick Springs Hotel in French Lick. The town has been a health spa since the eighteenth century due to the high mineral concentration of the waters.

51

The Atheneum in New Harmony was designed by Richard Meier.

Above: The Indiana War Memorial in Indianapolis. Constructed of Indiana limestone and granite, it is dedicated to Indiana citizens who gave their lives in the two World Wars and the Korean and Vietnam conflicts.

Opposite: The State Capitol of Indiana in Indianapolis. Located between Washington and Ohio Streets and Capitol and Senate Avenues, this Corinthian structure with its copper dome is built of Indiana limestone.

A Land of
Commerce

alterations

Chef Salad Bowls
SALAD BOWL HAM   2.00 2.50
SALAD BOWL TURKEY   2.00 2.50
SALAD BOWL SHRIMP   2.00 2.50
COKE · DIET · COKE · ICE TEA · MILK .50

Stews
BEEF STEW   2.00 2.50
SEAFOOD CHOWDER   2.00 2.50
CHICKEN · DUMPLINGS   2.00 2.50
CHILI CON CARNE   2.00 2.50
COKE · ICE TEA · MILK .50

OPEN for LUNCH
11:00 til 2:00
MON. THRU FRI.

A Land of Commerce

When most people think of Indiana commerce, they think of small stores and small factories. Nothing could be farther from the truth. It has had some hits and misses, but it is now an industrial giant.

Never mind that Wilbur Wright moved to Ohio, just think what would have happened if Henry Ford had not invented the production line—Indiana would be automobile maker to the world. At one time or another, automobiles were pouring out of the factories in the state—the Haynes and Apperson in Kokomo; the National, Premiere, Waverly Electric, Empire, Marion, Cole, Henderson, Parry, Pathfinder, Marmon, Lafayette, Stutz American Underslung and Auburn in Indianapolis; the Cord and Auburn in Auburn; the Studebaker in South Bend. In all, 56 Indiana towns turned out 246 different makes of cars.

The huge steel mills of the Calumet Region started taking form in 1906 when the United States Steel Corporation built mills so big that a new town, Gary, was established just to house the workers. The huge oil refining industry, also in the Calumet Region, began in 1889, when Standard Oil built a refinery in Whiting.

One of the little known contributions of Indiana to American commerce is in, of all things, the fashion industry. Bill Blass was born in Fort Wayne, Halston (Roy Halston Frowick) grew up in Evansville and Norell (Norman Levenson) was born in Noblesville.

Some of the other industries in the state produce aircraft engines, automobile parts, drugs, electronic equipment, paper products, telephones, aluminum, farm machinery, prefabricated houses, musical instruments, school buses, recreation vehicles, furniture, pottery, hardware and tools, bedding, pumps, railroad equipment, marine engines, canned goods and glass, foundry, leather and rubber products.

Agriculture, of course, is still an important industry in Indiana. The chief crops are corn, wheat, soybeans and hay, and as far as livestock is concerned, hogs, pigs, sheep and poultry lead the list. Other outdoor industries that are prominent are lumbering coal, sand, gravel and stone. There is also some commercial fishing and there are active ports east of Gary to accomodate the iron ore vessels that deliver the raw material for the steel mills.

Top: Steel-making in the Calumet Region uses oxygen furnaces.
Left: The farmers in Indiana have always needed their mills for grinding grain. This is the old Bonneyville Mill in Bristol.

Previous spread: Inside the City Market in Indianapolis. This renovated marketplace at 222 East Market Street was constructed in 1886. It features fresh meat, dairy, bakery and fruit stands as well as restaurants.

Above: The Springs Valley Electric Railroad Trolley at French Lick. It operates out of the old Monon Railroad station at the site of an old French trading post with its nearby salt lick.

Below: The Auburn-Cord-Duesenberg Museum in Auburn contains more than 130 of these and other classic cars, located in the original showroom of the Auburn Automobile Company.

Above: The *Belle of Louisville*, the old sternwheel riverboat, photographed on the Ohio River at Madison. In the middle of the nineteenth century, Madison was largest city in the state—5000 people.

Below: Old canal boats pulled by horses still travel along the Whitewater Canal at Metamora—but only for tourists. Canals were important in nineteenth century Indiana, for transporting goods and people.

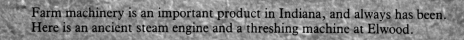

Farm machinery is an important product in Indiana, and always has been.
Here is an ancient steam engine and a threshing machine at Elwood.

Above: The interior of the 1900 John A Hook Drug Store in Nashville. This is a restoration of a turn-of-the-century pharmacy, with its original furnishings, drugstore antiques and soda fountain—the malted milks are wonderful.

Left: The Colgate Clock, located atop the Colgate-Palmolive plant in Jeffersonville, is the second largest clock in the world, measuring 40 feet in diameter.

Right: The massive pylons on the largest power line in the world span Indiana from North to South.

Opposite: A scene at the Selmer factory in Elkhart. Approximately 50 percent of the nation's band instruments are manufactured in 15 factories in the town. It all happened when a local grocer who was a cornetist injured his lip and invented a rubber mouthpiece. He received so many requests for his invention that he set up a cornet factory in 1875.

A Land of
Education

A Land of **Education**

Hardly had the Indiana Territory been established in 1800 than Hoosiers began to think about providing education for their young people. In 1801 the Jefferson Academy was founded—later to become Vincennes University, the oldest university west of the Allegheny Mountains. In 1816, Indiana became the first state to provide in its constitution for a state-wide system of free public schools. By the time that the state legislature got around to establishing taxes for these schools in 1849, nearly every township had a log schoolhouse built by the parents of the schoolchildren, with at least one teacher who was paid by the parents. The parents took turns providing a home for the schoolmaster or schoolmarm.

New Harmony schools had the first classes in the country in which boys and girls were taught together, one of the first nursery schools and perhaps the first shop classes, in which students were taught engraving, lithography and printing. In 1900, Bluffton, under the guidance of William Wirt, started the platoon school plan in which every child had a curriculum that combined study, play and work. Today, there are 2540 elementary and secondary schools in the state and 66 institutions of higher learning. These colleges and universities range from the mammoth Indiana University (80,000 students statewide, founded in 1820) and Purdue University (45,000 students statewide, founded in 1869), through distingushed religious-affiliated schools such as the University of Notre Dame (9000 students, founded in 1842) and Valparaiso University (4000 students, founded in 1859) to excellent small liberal arts colleges such as Depauw University (2500 students, founded in 1837) and Wabash College (800 students, founded in 1832).

The first public subscription library in the state opened in Vincennes in 1807. In 1816 a state law was passed that provided for county libraries. Some of the distinguished special libraries in the state are the Old Cathedral Library in Vincennes—the oldest—with some books dating from the 1400s, and the Lilly Library at Indiana University with its outstanding collection of American and English literature and its Gutenberg Bible. Some outstanding museums are the Children's Museum in Indianapolis and the Lincoln Museum in Fort Wayne.

Top: The Indianapolis Museum of Art contains comprehensive collections of primitive art, French, American and Oriental art, medieval and Renaissance art, French, English and Italian decorative art.
Left: The piano room of the Howard Steamboat Museum in Jeffersonville.

Previous spread: St Meinrad Archabbey and Seminary, founded in 1854.

Opposite: The old Student Building on the beautiful wooded campus of Indiana University at Bloomington. Founded in 1820, it is the oldest major state university west of the Allegheny Mountains.

Above: The Administration Building of the University of Notre Dame with its glorious golden dome. Inside are the Columbus murals of Luigi Gregori, once a portrait painter at the Vatican Museum in the 1860s.

Above: The solar greenhouse of the Hayes Regional Arboretum at Richmond.
Left: The Brown County Historical Museum in Nashville is located in an 1845 pioneer log cabin.
Center Top: The Northern Indiana Historical Society Museum in South Bend.

Top far left: Purdue University in West Lafayette.
Bottom far left: The East School at Depauw University.
Overleaf: The entrance to the Children's Museum in Indianapolis.

Welcome to The C

No food or drink
in museum

OUT

A Land of Recreation

A Land of **Recreation**

As far as recreation is concerned, Indiana has something for everyone. For hikers, campers and picnickers there are the Indiana Dunes National Lakeshore and the Hoosier National Forest, plus 19 beautiful state parks, 18 stunning state forests and 16 striking state fish and wildlife areas. For swimmers, boaters and fishermen, to the state forests, state fish and wildlife areas and state parks, can be added hundreds of lakes and the nine state reservoirs. For skiers, there are six ski areas.

For professional sports lovers, Indianapolis has it all—baseball with the Indianapolis Indians in the summer, football with the Indianapolis Colts in the fall, and basketball with the Indiana Pacers and hockey with the Indianapolis Checkers in the winter and spring.

College and university sporting events abound. Indiana boasts two members of the Big Ten Conference in Indiana University and Purdue University and one of the top independents in Notre Dame. Plus that, most of the state's 63 smaller institutions field teams in many sports. But perhaps the spectator sport that Hoosiers love the most is high school basketball—the 'Hoosier Hysteria.' There have been some high school gyms that hold as many spectators as there are people in the town, and getting a ticket to the Indiana State High School Athletic Association Basketball Tournament held in Indianapolis each March is almost an impossibility.

But the most famous annual event in Indiana is the 500-mile Memorial Day auto race in Indianapolis. With as many as 200,000 spectators it may be the most heavily attended single sporting event in the United States.

For relaxing recreational amusement there are the annual festivals, which happen the year around, beginning with the Creole King Ball in Vincennes in January. There are the Redbud-Dogwood Hayride in Nashville, the Round Barn Festival and the Trail of Courage Rendezvous in Rochester, the Apple Blossom Festival in Brown County, the Festival of the Golden Rain Tree in New Harmony, the Hillsdale Rose Festival, the Strawberry Festival in New Albany, the Summer Festival in Michigan City, the Circus City Festival in Peru, and many more.

Top: The Indiana University Hoosiers in a Big Ten football game versus Ohio State's Buckeyes in Memorial Stadium on the Bloomington campus.
Left: The Hoosier Dome in Indianapolis—home of the Indianapolis Colts.

Previous spread: Swimming in Lake Michigan in the Indiana Dunes State Park. The white sand beaches can accomodate thousands of swimmers and sun bathers.

Above: Hot air balloons take off at the Summer Festival in Anderson. Held in mid-June, the festival also features the White River Run, parachutists, an aviation show and a parade.

Opposite top: The annual Whitewater Canoe Race near Connorsville takes place on two days in late September. The distance is ten miles—from Laurel to Brookville—and the canoes travel both on the Whitewater River and the old Whitewater Canal, through one of the most scenic areas of Indiana where working locks, aqueducts and canal boat rides can be found. Along the way is the Whitewater Canal State Monument.

Right: The Little 500 Bicycle Race that is held each April on the Indiana University Bloomington Campus—an event with which the millions of moviegoers who saw the film *Breaking Away* are certainly familiar. The picture, starring Dennis Christopher, was shot in Bloomington in 1978. The race was begun by students in the late 1940s as a way to raise money for charity. Relay bicycle teams represented the various fraternities and men's dormitories, and they rode their old Schwinn bikes. Today they are more serious about the whole thing—going into concentrated training with expensive racing bikes.

Above: The toboggan run at Pokagon State Park near Angola.
Below: A view of the 500-mile Memorial Day auto race at the Speedway.
Below right: 'Hoosier Hysteria' in action. A game between Tippecanoe Valley of Mentone (in white) and Whitco of South Whitley.

Right: Turkey Run State Park near Marshall is a naturalist's heaven. It contains 2382 acres of beautiful virgin woods, canyons and streams. Named for a spot where wild turkeys once came to roost (and run), it offers facilities for canoeing, hiking, horseback riding, swimming and camping.

A Land of
People

A Land of **People**

Ethnically and religiously, Indiana is a true melting pot. The French, moving in from Canada and across the Great Lakes, were the first Europeans to explore the territory, and they set up the settlement of Vincennes, which began as a trading post in 1732. However, little remains today of French culture except the names of some communities such as La Porte, Terre Haute and Lafontaine.

By the second half of the eighteenth century, control had passed to the British and settlers from the eastern colonies were beginning to filter in, coming down the Ohio and across Kentucky. After the Revolutionary War, the trickle become a stready stream, many of the settlers being former soldiers who had been given land grants in lieu of pay. They cleared fields and built pioneer settlements.

In 1800, when the Indiana Territory was created with Vincennes as its capitol, Indiana contained about 5000 people; ten years later the number was about 25,000.

Among the settlers at this time were thousands of immigrants from Europe. The Swiss moved in to work the forests and manufacture furniture. They named Switzerland County and the little settlement of Tell City was named for their national hero. The Germans became bankers and brewers and civic leaders, developing the cities of Indianapolis and Terre Haute. First the Germans, then the Scots tried their hands at communal living in New Harmony. There was, however, only a small amount of emigration from the Spanish-speaking world, so it is hard to find a reason for the naming of such towns as Valparaiso and Mexico, which is but a few miles from Peru.

The first established settlers' religion was Roman Catholicism, and the first organized parish was at Vincennes, founded in 1749. When the British arrived, the Church of England and Methodism became prominent in the state. The Germans brought Lutheranism, the Swiss Calvinism and many others brought Fundamentalism. At one time the community of Ligonier was almost completely Jewish, but most of the farmers there moved away to engage in commerce closer to Chicago and Indianapolis. There is also a large Amish area and Richmond is a Quaker settlement. But in spite of this diversity, all the people are still Hoosiers.

Top: There is something for everyone at the Summer Festival in Anderson. Here a small jazz combo recalls the old days of Hoagy Carmichael and Eddie Condon.
Left: Hoosiers relaxing at Stone's Tavern at Ligonier, which dates back to 1839, having served as a stagecoach stop, school, tavern and courthouse.

Previous spread: The Fiddlers' Gathering at Lafayette. Musicians from all over the country gather to play their instruments and hold jam sessions.

WE MARCH SO T
CHILDREN O
ORAK-HAM
ORAK
POTENTATE
TEMPLE

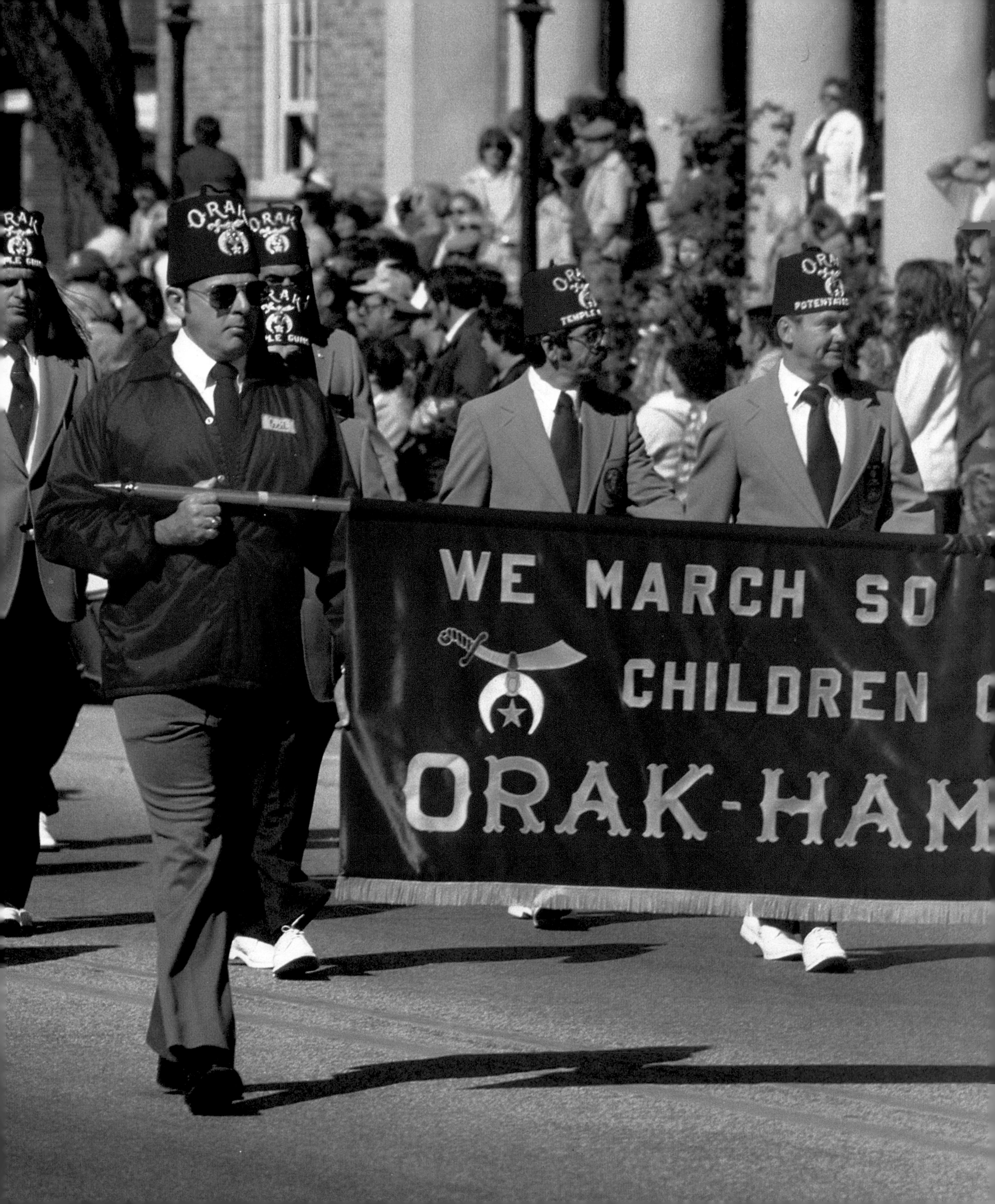

The Shriners are an important civic and social organization in Indiana. Here, members of the Orak Temple from Hammond march in a parade in Valparaiso.

Left: A woman cards wool by hand at Historic Fort Wayne, a reconstruction of the fort as it was during the 1815-19 period. Also in the fort are artifacts of the history of Indiana, and possessions of General 'Mad' Anthony Wayne, the hero of the Battle of Fallen Timbers, and Chief Little Turtle of the Miami Indians, who lost the battle.

Above: Hundreds attend the Arts Festival—The Chautauqua of the Arts—in Madison. Held in September, it features working artists and craftsmen displaying goods.
Overleaf: People come to meditate at the beautiful Grotto of Our Lady of Lourdes on the Notre Dame Campus in South Bend.

Above: A clown makes up for the annual Circus City Festival in Peru with its parade and amateur circus. Indiana was once the hub of the circus world. Peru had the largest circus winter quarters in the world—home to the huge Hagenback-Wallace–Circus, and a few miles up the road, Rochester was the winter home of the Cole Brothers Circus.

Left: Wandering through the pumpkin patch at Stonycreek Farm near Noblesville. Each year the farm, which features horse-drawn hay rides, nature trails, a petting corral, playgrounds, picnicking and fishing, is host to the Pumpkin Harvest Festival.

Below: The Fourth of July Parade at the Conner Prairie Pioneer Settlement near Noblesville. Owned and operated by Earlham College in Richmond, the settlement contains 25 buildings, including William Conner's brick mansion (1823).

Overleaf: 'When I dream about the moonlight on the Wabash/Then I long for my Indiana home.'